Growing Old Disgracefully

poems by

Elizabeth Marchitti

Finishing Line Press
Georgetown, Kentucky

Growing Old Disgracefully

Copyright © 2017 by Elizabeth Marchitti
ISBN 978-1-63534-292-5 First Edition
All rights reserved under International and Pan-American Copyright Conventions.
No part of this book may be reproduced in any manner whatsoever without written permission from the publisher, except in the case of brief quotations embodied in critical articles and reviews.

ACKNOWLEDGMENTS

The following poems have been published in these journals:

On the Subject of Gabardine: *The Paterson Literary Review*
Halleluiah: *The Paterson Literary Review*
I Am Not White Bread: *The Paterson Literary Review*
Family Resemblances: *The Paterson Literary Review*
And These Are My Vices: *Lips*
Mother's Snuggies: *The Paterson Literary Review*

Publisher: Leah Maines

Editor: Christen Kincaid

Cover Art and Design: John Marchitti

Author Photo: John Marchitti

Printed in the USA on acid-free paper.
Order online: www.finishinglinepress.com
also available on amazon.com

Author inquiries and mail orders:
Finishing Line Press
P. O. Box 1626
Georgetown, Kentucky 40324
U. S. A.

Table of Contents

Beware 1

When I Met My Muse 2

July At The Totowa Pool 3

Beach Ball Ballet 4

I Had To Have My Long Beach Island Fix 5

The Great Falls 7

Before The Chill 9

Autumn Song 10

Halleluiiah 11

On The Subject of Gabardine 13

Family Resemblances 14

Mother's Snuggies 15

I Am Not White Bread 16

Elegy for My Youth 19

And These Are My Vices 20

I Think I Should Give Up Exercise 21

How to Be Happy 23

BEWARE

Senior Citizens,
we are everywhere,
be very afraid—

Driving slowly on the Parkway,
not even looking before switching lanes,
holding social get-togethers
in the aisles of supermarkets,
unconcerned about blocking traffic—

Senior Citizens,
we are everywhere,
be afraid, be very afraid—

WHEN I MET MY MUSE
After reading William Stafford's "When I Met My Muse"

I met my muse one sunny day
as I sat on my deck.
He hopped onto the railing
and he chirped at me,
as if to say,
"Isn't it about time you wrote a poem?"

Mr. Sparrow had been building a nest
in the birdhouse we call The Hotel.
It has four apartments
and little birds like to live there.
Mrs. Sparrow was in the nest,
perhaps re-arranging the "furniture."

I tossed him some peanuts,
which he quietly ate,
leaving none for the resident squirrel,
who came too late.
Better luck next time,
I said to him.

I do admire the way
he sits back on his haunches
and nibbles nuts, holding
them in his tiny paws,
which so resemble human hands.
Perhaps I should re-think—
Is the friendly squirrel
also my muse?
My muses neither hum nor buzz,
like William Stafford's does.
Still, I'm glad for each chirp or chatter,
reminder: it's time to write.

JULY AT THE TOTOWA POOL
6:00 P.M.

I sit alone enjoying the warmth
of the worn wooden picnic bench.
On the opposite side of the parking lot
a mockingbird repeats his repertoire
of birdsongs.
Sparrows hop close, snatching cracker crumbs.
They like whole wheat, and so do I.

Catbird comes by, his royal grey beauty,
his perky dark tail always
a pleasure to behold.
He does not speak.
Grackles stride in the grass,
the dignified, haughty walk
all blackbirds seem to own,
then fly up to the trees,
"*chek, chek, chek*-ing" with loud voice.

While sparrows, silent, hop and eat,
and mockingbird re-iterates his song.

BEACH BALL BALLET

Four beach balls dance
on the surface of the pool,
stay together like quadruplets
cling to the edge
as if they are afraid to swim.

When the breeze picks up
they dance across the water
along the pool's edge, turning, turning—
cocoa-cola beach ball, red and white
one blue, green and yellow,
one red, yellow and white,
one blue, white and orange—

Isn't it lucky that
I do not write in rhyme—
blue, white and orange,
red, yellow and white,
blue, green and yellow
ballet of the beach balls,
dancing in the breeze.

I HAD TO HAVE MY LONG BEACH ISLAND FIX
September, 2015

Stay at the Buccaneer Motel in Spray Beach,
with the perfect view of the bay.
If we only stayed two overnights,
I promised not to be greedy.
and want more.
I would have the sight of the bay,
seagulls, kayakers, sailboats—
then climb up and down the dune
to the sandy beach—enjoy
the sound of breaking waves.

I wouldn't try to swim in the sea,
but be content to watch the waves,
to smell the fragrance of salt air,
to know the calm that seashore brings.

If there was time, we'd walk along the channel
where bay enters ocean by Old Barney,
the Barnegat Lighthouse. Never
a trip to Long Beach Island
without the drive to the lighthouse.

We did it all. I had three separate swims
In the Buccaneer's 80 degree pool,
one trip to the top of the dune
to watch and listen to the sea,
one scenic drive from Spray Beach
to the town of Barnegat Light, to Old Barney

John surprised me when
he said he would climb to the top,
as he had done so many times before,
while I sat below and waved.

On August 4th he'd had a stent installed,
On September 1st two more in one artery.
Should he climb those 217 steps
to the top of Old Barney?
I didn't think so.
But he did it with ease, testing
the success of the stent surgery.

Then we strolled the walkway
along the channel, where bay met ocean,
every minute of our two day stay—
:::::::::::::::::::::perfect.

THE GREAT FALLS
October 27, 2015

No rain for so long—
dry August, September, October—
We journey to the new park, called Mary Ellen Kramer Park,
behind the Passaic Falls ,as I knew it.
The Great Falls, its official name.
the Passaic River meanders
through Passaic, then Paterson,
flows to the Falls—
murmuring water falling
into the river below.
only in one or two places, now.

Bare rocks, tinted several colors,
have their own beauty,
carved as they were
from eons of water cascading
into the canyon, making it
deeper and deeper.

Ah, the sound of it,
the fragrance of water.
No mist. No Rainbows.
Not the Falls I remember.
We walk the old bridge over the chasm,
Repaired many times,
reborn many times

I remember the roar of the Falls
after a nor'easter.
No voices could be heard
over the sound.
The moving mist bathed us
in its benevolence,
always a rainbow over the Falls.

We wait for rain to restore
Its glory.

BEFORE THE CHILL
On the backyard deck

Hot sun. Cool breeze,
more like wind—sudden gusts.
Elm leaves fly through air,
twirl, dance, flutter down like snow.

This tall tree I see
in my neighbor's yard,
with leaves like stars,
what is its name?

Green leaves tipped with gold,
a few faded to brown .
If I could paint, I would:
portrait of a tree with autumn colors.

Decorative windmill turns
faster and faster,
three wheels of color: red, yellow, green.
Each turns in opposite directions.

I love my deck most days of the year.
Will I bundle up and sit here
In falling snow?
       I might

I WANT TO SING AN AUTUMN SONG
October 2015

Sitting on the deck in warm November sun,
watching jet trails in a sky of brilliant blue,
No clouds.   No clouds at all,
just a breeze, so cool, so cool,
looking at that tree, so red, so tall.
leaves don't seem to fall, but twirl and spin
and dance and sing,
a rustling in the autumn breeze.

Now I begin to sing my song,
love the breeze, the trees, warm sun that shines.
In the autumn of my life,
 my autumn song.

My friend Vicky, singer/songwriter, guitar player, accompanied this poem with appropriate music at The Ant Bookstore in Clifton, N.J. on November 21, 2015

HALLELUIAH
(Mary Oliver spelled it this way—alternative: Hallelujah)

I have fallen in love
with my hometown at last.
It's something that grew
over the years.
I have, after all,
been living here since 1966.
At first, I missed my "penthouse,"
that third floor apartment
under an almost flat roof,
hot in summer, cold in winter,
where we could see the sky
through the spaces
in the wainscotting
of the kitchen walls.

My children missed the noise,
even the dirt of the city,
their friends at school,
the possibility
of walking to church
and to the library.

I missed my three clotheslines
and my downstairs neighbor, Angela,
my view of the sky
from my back porch
and my imagining
of the Passaic Falls,
off there in the distance,
beyond the rooftops.

I learned to love where I live.
The song of the birds
no longer awakens me
in early morning.
Sparrows have become my muses.
I delight in the sight
of the tufted titmouse
and his quick visit to the feeder.

I find the Totowa Public Library
a haven, and a quick trip
to Barnes and Noble
in nearby Woodland Park
a blessing.

I love the traffic lights
on Union Boulevard,
and the drivers who use Dewey Ave.
as a shortcut during rush hour.
I love the schools
where my children grew up,
the maple trees that used
to shade Dewey Ave.,
and the pear trees
that bloom there now
in the spring.

I have fallen in love
with my home town,
at last.

ON THE SUBJECT OF GABARDINE
From Gabardine, by Ted Kooser:
To sit in sunlight with other old men, hands curled in our laps . . .
like birds that now and then fly up with our words . . .
casting a shadow over our pants legs, gabardine . . .

Old women don't wear gabardine,
well, maybe if it's polyester
and comes in a dark color.
We don't sit in sunlight
with other old women,
legs uncrossed and
hands on our knees.
We're probably at home,
emailing our grandchildren in college,
or maybe browsing in Barnes & Noble,
looking for that Barbara Kingsolver novel
that we somehow missed,
or that book of poems
by some old poet, now gone,
who had a lot to say to us,
or maybe having tea with old friends,
gesturing with our busy old hands
to emphasize a point.

FAMILY RESEMBLANCES

Admiring my granddaughter Sarah-Ann's curly hair,
I wonder—where did it come from?
Yes, her mom, my daughter, has curly hair,
but her sisters do not.
Yes, my son, her brother, had thick, curly hair,
but now, he's fifty, and his curls are gone,
his brush cut thin, some bare scalp showing.
Still handsome, of course, and I remember
my husband's Aunt Kate used to say,
the more the heritage mix, the more beautiful
the children. Armenian, Irish, Dutch, and Italian,
Americans all. Nothing said about curly hair.

My friend Gerry used to tell me
that baldness was inherited
from the mother's side of the family.
How to explain Dad's fairly thick hair
when he died at eighty-two?
How to explain my Mom's soft grey waves
when she died at ninety-seven?
How to explain my almost curly hair,
wild as a haystack every morning,
begging to be combed over and over
till it looks right?

MOTHER'S SNUGGIES

My mother never wore slacks.
When she was over ninety-five,
and in the nursing home,
she wore sweat pants and tops,
pretty colored ones my sister
and I bought for her.

But earlier, when she used
to walk to Christ Church
for the mid-week service,
no matter how chilly the weather,
my mother never wore slacks.

She wore warm woolen skirts
with her nylons and sensible shoes.
Underneath her skirt, she wore snuggies,
those warm cotton underpants
with legs that came down
to her knees, almost.

Apparently they kept her quite warm.
When she lived with my husband and me,
in her early nineties, she needed new snuggies.
They were very hard to find.
Once you are old, the world forgets
that you need things you were used to.

I finally found them in a mail order catalog,
so my mother could be warm
on a cold winter Sunday,
when I drove us to church,
me in my warm velour slacks,
Mother in her snuggies.

I AM NOT WHITE BREAD
With apologies to ethnic writers everywhere

All right. My skin is fair.
I was a blonde once, when I was four.
All right. I'm pretty much white.
But that doesn't make me bland.
That doesn't make me boring or unemotional.
I'm just as volatile as the next guy,
and by guy, I mean woman.

My grandfather, my mother's father,
was Armenian. He came to the USA
after his first wife died, leaving
his son behind with relatives.
He was a weaver in the broad silk,
in Paterson, the Silk City,
My grandmother, my mother's mother,
was Irish. She came to the USA alone,
at the age of sixteen, to become a cook
for a well-to-do American family.

I don't know where they met.
I only remember the tale Mother told,
how the Armenian ladies wanted
to loan Grandma some of their gold jewelry,
but Grandma didn't care about such adornments.
Grandma baked bread once a week.
She gave me warm buttered bread
with weak tea to drink. I was five.
Grandma died when I was six.
Grandpa baked bread, too.
It was brown and flat, like pita.
Mother called it "poppa's bread."

My father was a Hollander,
through and through,
raised by his Dutch grandmother,
after his mother died
in the flu epidemic of 1918.
Dad was tall. Mom was short.
They met at Warner Woven Label.
Dad was a weaver. Mom was a quill winder.
Are they lost arts? Or do they still exist
in China, Bangladesh, and Jordan?

My father's father made him quit
school after the eighth grade.
He was the eldest, his help
was needed at home.
My mother hated school,
she was glad to leave
as soon as she turned fourteen.
Strangely enough, they both
loved to read, and so do I.

I'm a depression baby.
My parents married in 1929,
I was born in l931.My father was working
four days a week
There was no such thing
as health insurance, but my father
had a job. We survived.
My mother used to say,
we don't have a lot of money,
but we have a lot of fun.
We did, putting puzzles together,

playing monopoly,
singing "It's a long, long way
to Tipperary" on the way
to Greenwood Lake Beach in summer.
We paid by the carload.

Later, when my sister and I were grown,
we gathered at Mom and Dad's
for Sunday supper with our children.
The talk around the table
grew very loud.   We wondered
what their quiet neighbors thought.
We were not fighting, just discussing.

I am not white bread.
I am a mutt, the product
of a blessed mixed heritage.
History has shaped me.
I am not bland.
I am just as unpredictable
as the next woman.

ELEGY FOR MY YOUTH

It's gone a long time ago
Yet I remember all those things
I no longer do:
Climb trees
Take long walks
Dive into a lake
Swim in the ocean
Play badminton in the street
Skate on frozen ponds
Run up the stairs
Knit argyle socks
Sew dresses for my daughters
Type papers for my son

Once young, strong and slender
I dreamed of my future
Now it's my past
I have no regrets
Entitled to be old
fat, wrinkled and grey
I can still read books
I can still dream.

AND THESE ARE MY VICES

I talk too much
I get off on a tangent
make a short story long
I put off doing things
I don't want to do
in favor of reading
I read too much
My excuse: I read
The Smithsonian and *The Atlantic*
to educate myself
to learn about the world
I read novels to hide in my shell.
I'm vain. I like bright lipstick
green eyeshadow
and pretty fingernails
I scrape off the polish
with my teeth as I read
I keep promising myself to lose weight
but can't resist a chocolate chip cookie

Nevertheless
I am kind to small animals
birds
      and some people too

I THINK I SHOULD GIVE UP EXERCISE

I think I have given up exercise
unless you count the trip
from the living room
where I sit, feet up, reading,
to the kitchen, where
my new washer/dryer hums
doing its job with grace
Silence tells me the dryer
has stopped
It's time to fold the laundry.

I stand to do that,
make a neat pile
of towels and t-shirts,
return to my lounge chair
and my novel, feet up

I think I have given up exercise
unless you count trips
to J.C. Penney's, Barnes & Noble,
or the Totowa Public Library
unless you count the long walk
down the aisle at the Paper Mill Playhouse

Or the short walk, after John has parked our car,
to the Montclair Public Library
or the Hamilton Club in Paterson,
to attend poetry readings.
I think I have given up exercise,
unless you count
how happily I jump up
and walk to the podium
to read at various Open Mikes.

Soon I will swim
in the heated indoor pool
at the Bird-In-Hand Family Inn
in Amish Country, Pennsylvania
This is so easy, so much fun.
Can it be called exercise?

In June I will swim
in the outdoor heated pool
at the Beachcomber Resort
in Avalon, Three Mile Island.
This is too easy
to be called exercise.

I will exercise my brain
by reading Murikami,
Alice Hoffman
and the poems of those
poets I love.

It's time to slow down,
Relax, to grow old
        disgracefully.

HOW TO BE HAPPY

Read a good book.
Discover a new author.
Write a poem.
Drink hot tea with honey.
Talk to daughters on the phone.
Send email to grandchildren.
Make a special dinner
for your husband.
Thank him every day
for all he does for you.
Remember how it felt to be young.
Be grateful to be old,
                not dead.

Elizabeth Marchitti is married to John, her personal Patron of the Artist. They have four grown children and eight grandchildren. She has been writing poetry for many years, and occasionally a short story or an essay. Her work has been published in *Lips, The Paterson Literary Review, The Journal of New Jersey Poets, Sensations Magazine*, and some small local journals.

In 2010, her poem "The Music Tree" won First Prize in the annual Art, Photography and Poetry Exhibition at St. Catherine's of Ringwood. She also judged the competition in 2015 with two other New Jersey poets.

In 2011, her mini-chapbook, "In Praise of Stillness," won first prize in the contest sponsored by Sugarland Press of Texas. She has been known to read in local Open Mike events, as she loves to read her poems aloud, and interact with the audience. She has been a member of a small group called Café Poets for a number of years, and also leads another, known as Writing for Fun, at the Totowa Library. She wishes to thank her poet/friends for their continual inspiration, especially Maria Mazziotti Gillan and Laura Boss for their continuing workshops.

Perhaps she should also thank Pablo Neruda, William Stafford, Wendell Berry, Ted Kooser, Mary Oliver and Naomi Shihab Nye for their inspiring poetry. Art saves us.

www.ingramcontent.com/pod-product-compliance
Lightning Source LLC
LaVergne TN
LVHW041522070426
835507LV00012B/1748